Remnants
Restante
Reste

Remnants
Restante
Reste

Annette Snyckers

First published by Modjaji Books 2018

www.modjajibooks.co.za
info@modjajibooks.co.za

© Annette Snyckers

ISBN (print): 978-1-928215-59-2
ISBN (ebook): 978-1-928215-60-8

Layout and design by Fire and Lion
Cover artwork by Annette Snyckers
Author photograph by Peter Snyckers

Contents

For Fritz, who stands beside me

Tong

Ek vou my tong
om my taal, versigtig –
want sy hou haar
soms opsy.
Ek flonker mos flikkers
vir die ander
hulle klanke bekoor my,
hulle woorde verlei.

Ek ontdek ander ekke
in vreemde tale –
saam reis ons
na verre lande,
maar tuis
vou ek weer my tong
om my taal, gemaklik –
sy proe soos my plek.

Tongue

I fold my tongue
around my language, carefully –
because she keeps herself
apart sometimes.
I flirt with the others
their sounds charm me,
their words seduce.

I discover other selves
in strange languages –
together we travel
to far countries,
but at home
I fold my tongue
around my language again, with ease –
she tastes like my place.

Zunge

Ich falte meine Zunge
um meine Sprache, vorsichtig –
denn sie hält sich
manchmal abseits.
Ich kokettiere mit den andern
ihre Laute bezaubern mich,
ihre Worte verführen.

Ich entdecke mich mehrmals
in fremden Sprachen –
wir reisen zusammen
in ferne Länder,
aber zuhause
falte ich wieder meine Zunge
um meine Sprache, mühelos –
sie schmeckt wie meine Heimat.

Take Note

I am drawn to making lists and writing notes,
wrapping up in words my every day
to record the mundane,
of who had whooping cough when
and the miraculous,
of who passed matric without opening a book.
Also all the sad days when pets died
and the mad elation at the birth of a child.
My life is packed in little black books
in which I can check when it was
you wrote the car off one night
and the hospital called.
I can find things long forgotten,
like the name of every cat I ever loved
and how much I paid
for that dress I bought in Paris.
The time the snake slithered down the passage,
how the bushbaby sat on my head
and groomed me every night,
the time it snowed in September,
how you turned blue from that allergy,
even the time I swallowed a fly.

Not knowing how,
how to live this life,
some dates stayed blank.

Clipped

On those days
I ran about the garden
like a wild foal,
my father was convinced
that little devils nested
in my mane.

White sheet draped
over small shoulders,
I was made to sit
so he could snip
to exorcise the sprites
who whispered in my ears.

I emerged bobbed,
cut straight,
in step.

Geknip

Op daardie dae
wat ek deur die tuin gehol het
soos 'n wilde vul,
was my pa oortuig
dat klein duiwels
nesgemaak het in my maanhare.

Wit laken gedrapeer
oor klein skouertjies,
is ek sitgemaak
dat hy kon snipper
om die geeste te besweer
wat in my ore gefluister het.

Ek het kortgeknip daar uitgekom,
reguit gesny,
in pas.

The Moth that Launched a Career

On Aunt Miem's kitchen wall
there was a moth – not a moth
that just sat there, the way moths
sometimes sit and drowse
under the warm glow of a lamp –
or a fluttering moth
that bumbles forth into the flame,
no, just a small drab moth
painted with care,
but trapped forever
on a greasy wall
above the kitchen table.
It looked content there
with my aunt and two cousins,
and never
fell in their soup.

I was seven,
crazy for that moth
and the unknown artist
I secretly adored.

Synaesthesia

At six or seven
I would close my eyes
and see them
as I thought everyone else
could see them –
not only in full colour,
but each with its own
quaint character.

Monday was not really blue,
but rather rosy,
Tuesday was the blue one, pale,
and Wednesday was canary yellow.
Thursday was the green day
and Friday fiery red.
Saturday was purple
and Sunday rather gray.

It would be dishonest to claim
that I could smell them too.

Catch

That holiday
when we camped
almost on the beach –
the lonely afternoons
drooped from the Milkwoods.
My parents slept and I,
in my bubble bathing suit,
I challenged the waves –
over and over
walls of liquid glass
rose up and I stood
until the very last moment,
just before
the wave would curl over
and crash down,
then I turned,
and ran as fast as I could
on spindly legs
like a sandpiper.

The thrill, the need
to outrun a living force
licking my heels –
sea smell,
gull cries,
my heart a hammer.

When my parents woke up,
we had tea and rusks.
I never told them
how fast I could run.

Bolt

On summer afternoons
when flies were lazy
and the hours lame,
I was supposed to lie down,
rest in my room –
when my mother took a nap,
all I wanted was out.

In the passage
creaking floorboards
lay waiting
to snap at my heels,
but I held my breath,
stepped over them,
and only exhaled
when I reached
the dining room.

Out, out,
over the fence
and into the veld –
crushed grass
and khaki bush,
turtle dove
and hoepoe,

sun
budding my wings.

The Final No

Many years ago
when my father feared
that his youngest daughter
would fall in love
with the spotlight,
he cleared his throat
and finally said no.

I was too small,
I did not have the words
to sway him –
all I could do
was climb the koppie
behind the house
and sob for hours
in the tall dry grass
until the kiewiet called me back
from Swan Lake to the winter veld.

No ballet pointes
to help me on my toes
no frilly tutu,
no soaring music to lift me up.
How I would have flown.

But I'm toeing my father's line.

Language Lesson

My language was not hers,
misunderstandings rose like walls –
two women separated by words.
I wanted to reach her.

I took her language to my breast,
learnt to love it:
Mörike, Morgenstern,
Heine, Hesse...

Her language became mine –
it was essential to understand her:
because above all –
I loved her son.

Sprachstunde

Meine Sprache war nicht die Ihre,
Missverständnisse erhoben sich wie Wände –
zwei Frauen durch Worte getrennt.
Ich wollte zu ihr finden.

Ich nahm ihre Sprache an meine Brust,
lernte sie lieben:
Mörike, Morgenstern,
Heine, Hesse...

Ihre Sprache wurde die Meine –
notwendig war's sie zu verstehen:
denn über alles –
liebte ich ihren Sohn.

Strange Soil

First visit to Germany

Black-grey-white, winter –
my first visit, melancholy mist,
thoughts of terrible things
on the cold soil of the land.

The farm on the moor,
high oaks naked in the snow,
new relatives – shy,
my tongue still tripping.

Spring –
a walk to the lake,
on the pale sandy path
tiny black toads wriggle.

Among water lilies,
bulging and shrinking,
the throats of amorous frogs
croak in cadence – new life, new life.

In the dark forest,
when other birds already sleep,
I hear at last, insistent,
the voice of the nightingale –
so different from the harsh cries
of the hadedahs back home
at night.

Fremder Boden

Erster Deutschlandbesuch

Schwarz-grau-weiß, Winter –
mein erster Besuch, melancholischer Nebel,
Gedanken an Schreckliches
auf dem kalten Boden des Landes.

Der Hof in der Heide,
hohe Eichen nackt im Schnee,
neue Verwandte – scheu,
meine Zunge noch stolpernd.

Frühling –
Spaziergang zum See –
auf dem hellen Sandweg
wühlen winzig schwarze Kröten.

Zwischen Seerosen,
schwellend und schrumpfend
quaken die Kehlen der verliebten Frösche
im Takt – neues Leben, neues Leben.

Im dunklen Wald,
wenn andere Vögel schon schlafen,
höre ich endlich, beharrlich,
die Stimme der Nachtigall –
so anders als das grelle Geschrei
der Ibisse meiner Heimat
in der Nacht.

Firstborn

It was cold, a wet summer's day
in a far-off foreign country,
I had to wear a coat.
I see Klinik Hirslanden
on the hill, rain over the lake,
night falling and city lights below –
how wild waves of birthing shook me.

I remember your arrival,
how I could not sleep thereafter,
transformed, intoxicated,
all through the night I soared
above that dark expanse of water.

Erstgeboren

Es war kalt, ein nasser Sommertag
in einem fremden Land weit weg,
Ich musste einen Mantel tragen.
Ich sehe Klinik Hirslanden am Hang,
Regen über den See,
Einbruch der Nacht und Stadtlichter unten –
wie wilde Geburtswehen mich schüttelten.

Ich gedenke Deiner Ankunft,
wie ich nachher nicht schlafen konnte,
verwandelt, berauscht,
die ganze Nacht durch schwebte ich
über jene dunkle Weite des Wassers.

Husband

Your horse was brown,
not white,
that did not bother me
you held the reins, sat proud,
the sun played on your hair,
your eyes were kind.

I watch you,
playing with the children
of our children –
now you are the horse,
they the princes
and princesses
riding on your knee.

Ehemann

Dein Pferd war braun,
nicht weiß,
das hat mich nicht gestört
du hieltest die Zügel, saßest stolz,
die Sonne spielte auf deinem Haar,
deine Augen waren freundlich.

Ich beobachte dich
wie du mit den Kindern
unserer Kinder spielst –
jetzt bist du das Pferd,
sie sind die Prinzen
und Prinzessinnen
die auf deinem Knie reiten.

No Frills

This morning
you forgot your lunchbox
on the kitchen table.
Inside I found
two slices of rye,
two slices of cheese
unadorned
no red tomato,
no lettuce frill,
no mustard,
no dill.

Hungry post-war years
left their mark on you
perhaps it's now permissible
to add a carrot or two?

Afterthought:
There are men
who have tipped the other way
they strut around pot-bellied,
I prefer you.

The Mother of Boys

I've been a mother to silkworms
and white mice
to snakes and ferrets
to bunnies we could not
face feeding to the python
to lost teenagers
to lovesick girlfriends
and to you, all three of you.

Enough now, let's be friends.

Firsthand

Eyes can lie,
but hands reveal
through skin and sinew
veins and nails
grip and grasp
stroke and strike

how young, how old
how careful, how fearful
how kind, how cold
how tense

how tender.

Daddy's Helper

Your hands on wood,
(tongue between your lips)
and I – only a girl, not the son
who should be helping –
I sat and watched,
sometimes was allowed
to hold the end of the measuring tape –
I could not take my eyes off your hands,
how they caressed the wood,
held the paintbrush, concentration
furrowed on your forehead.

Because you believed
women's hands should not
handle implements,
tools and paintbrushes
(we would mess it up),
you never taught me.
I watched, and learned
to use my small hands
only later, when they grew
into a woman's hands,
my eyes to measure things
to within half a millimetre,
to plumb as straight and true
as a level.

↘

I paint in translucent layers
on canvas
the way you painted
walls and cupboards;
my hands get dirty
and I inhale, thrilled,
the smell of turpentine.
I have disobeyed you –

but I know that now,
you would not be angry.

Fur

My fingers are lost
in the fur of my dog,
it's warm against my skin,
it tickles my nose,
I breathe her in.

The silver-grey silk
of my cat catches the sun,
catches my breath –
she tolerates my kiss,
I breathe her in – captive.

I have kept another
soft animal in the dark –
on the days I crumple,
I take out the fur coat
from the cupboard –

I push my face into it,
I breathe her in – my mother.

Pelz

Meine Finger sind verloren
in dem Fell meiner Hündin,
es liegt warm an meiner Haut,
es kitzelt meine Nase,
ich atme sie ein.

Die silber-graue Seide
meiner Katze fängt die Sonne auf,
hält meinen Atem an –
sie toleriert meinen Kuss,
ich atme sie ein – bezaubert.

Ich habe ein anderes
weiches Tier in Dunkelheit gehalten –
an den Tagen wo ich knicke,
hole ich den Pelzmantel
aus dem Schrank –

Ich drücke ihn an meinem Gesicht,
ich atme sie ein – meine Mutter.

Om weg te vlieg

Nadat die somervure
haar uit haar huis
bokant Valsbaai gerook het,
het sy na my toe gekom,
in die stoel by die venster gesit
en vreemde stories vertel
van mense lank reeds dood,
stories van ons ouers
wat ek anders onthou het.

Sy wat elke blaar geken het
en selfs die kleinste blom
liefgehad het, wou nie
in die tuin stap nie – daar het
'n swaarte op haar bors gesit –
haar enkels was geswel,
haar asem kort,
sy het die bed geweier,
dis so moeilik om weer op te staan,
het sy gesê, nog nie bereid
om vir die dood te gaan lê nie.

Noudat jy weg is, is ek jammer
dat ek jou die gestyfde
bed met tralies nie kon spaar nie,
nie die kortaf verpleegsters nie,
nie die afskeid van jou huis nie.

↘

Ek wéét jy sou verkies het
om in jou grys stoel weg te raak
en saam met die Janfrederik
wat altyd by jou deur
kom krummels eet het,
weg te vlieg
oor die diep blou baai.

Remnants from a Cottage by the Sea

In a cupboard in the cellar,
invaded by more than mould,
is a box of fishing tackle all a-jumble,
twisted hooks and sinkers,
reminders of night-fishing expeditions
undertaken by the young boys of this house.
Late the lamp came over the dune,
brought into the kitchen
where, by its flickering light,
they slaughtered and consumed
the freshly-baked bread.

Years later, digging in a drawer
for thumb tacks and the scissors,
I find puzzle pieces, shells,
self-made cards for Christmas,
drawings of bunnies with long ears,
a witch upon her broom.

Early on the first morning
of the new millennium,
two children climbed
into bed with me –
outside the sea lay silver
so we pretended to be on a ship –

all of us so unprepared
for the rough passage ahead.

When We're Gone

The moon has plunged
behind the hill
the sun swum up
from the dark sea.

Our bed is bathed in light,
but it is bare
covered only by a sheet
against the dust.

Ash is swept from the grate
crumbs wiped from the table
the curtains are closed
the key turned in the lock.

The moon will grow and wane –
spiders and striped mice
ants and dustbunnies
will reclaim their domain.

The Swimmer

My heart beats faster
at the roar of the sea
at the slap of cold water
against my thighs
the hiss of bursting bubbles
and foam frothing
around my ears
the taste of salt
biting my lips.

Breath and sky
fish and bird
the tug of the deep
on my sun-brown body –

my small life.

Die swemmer

My hart klop vinniger
met die brul van die see,
met die klap van koue water
teen my dye
die sis van borrels wat bars
en skuim wat bruis
om my ore
die smaak van sout
wat byt aan my lippe.

Asem en lug
vis en voël
die pluk van die diep
aan my son-bruin lyf –

my klein lewe.

Never

Never in the days
when you marched on short, sturdy legs
through the wilderness
of our garden

never in the days
when summer sang in the high trees
and you sailed your boat
on the bird-bath

never in the days
of winter when we stayed inside
and you spread my silk scarves
to make a magic carpet

never in the days
before a birthday when I baked a cake
and you stood waiting
to lick the mixing bowl

not then,
not ever,
could I imagine
that you would live
just behind the bulge
of the mountain –

so close to me
under the same stars,
but
beyond the moon.

Night Vision

In the blackness of night
there was bright light
and people mulled about
in the strange place I stood –
I hovered around her,
but hung back,
I tried to get her attention –
a small bag of mementoes
unzipped in my hand.

I wanted to give her
those old silver coins,
anything from our past,
a symbol, something
she did not yet know
she might need later –
she was not interested
and left with friends.
I felt a fool for trying.
She was all grown-up.

Small Animal

The shabby space
where I kept looking for myself
was invaded by ants
blown by the wind –
many creatures lived there.

I dreamed of predators each night –
lion and leopard at my heels
and I running, running
until the small animal in me understood
it was only fleeing from itself.

In the therapist's green velvet chair
her words tasted like honey –
even lions like it.

Kleines Tier

Der schäbige Ort
wo ich mich selber ständig suchte
war von Ameisen überfallen
vom Winde verweht –
viele Kreaturen lebten dort.

Ich träumte jede Nacht von Raubtieren –
Löwen und Leoparden hinter mir her
und ich rannte, rannte
bis das kleine Tier in mir verstand
dass es bloß vor sich selber floh.

In dem grünen Samtstuhl der Therapeutin
smeckten ihre Worte wie Honig –
sogar von Löwen beliebt.

The Striped Sofa

I still see the striped sofa
standing in a pool of sunlight
by the sash window –
on that terrible day
when I lay down in its lap
and tried to untangle tomorrows
from yesterdays. I lifted my eyes
to the mountain and wondered
where my help would come from.

Sky drenched my eyes with blue,
trees lay their fluttery green fingers
on my forehead and
the mountain stood its ground,
resplendent in purples and greys.

Das gestreifte Sofa

Ich sehe das gestreifte Sofa
am Schiebefenster
in einem See des Sonnenlichts –
an dem schrecklichen Tag
als ich mich in seinen Schoß legte,
und versuchte morgen von gestern
zu entwirren. Ich hob meine Augen
zum Berge auf und fragte
woher meine Hilfe kommen würde.

Der Himmel badete meine Augen im Blau,
die Baüme legten ihre flatternden
grünen Finger auf meine Stirn und
der Berg stand unerschütterlich,
strahlend in Purpur und Grau.

Question Marks

Let me not wear black today,
or florals for that matter – although
the star jasmine twinkles on the trellis
and showers the morning with perfume,
although billowy roses are in bloom,
and the privet smells like lazy days
in that garden below the koppie
when I was a girl, dreaming
dreams that reached
for days still far
ahead.

I arrive in the future
each morning – I am here,
unsure, travel-weary and dusty –
so let me unpack a clean white shirt,
and be blessed by its crisp coolness.
Although this day has already drawn
black question marks on my skin,
let me begin with a fresh
blank canvas
let me wear
white.

The Visitor

Like some unloved relative
who stands at your door
and rings the bell
on a beautiful morning
when you have other plans,
the uninvited visitor knows
you will have to show your face
and let him in.

He then sits back,
this bringer of nasty news,
tells you just where you went wrong
watches you run to and fro,
attending to his every need
while you hope and pray
that he might leave
just as suddenly as he came.

But trouble seldom does –
he's come prepared
his bag is in the car.

He likes to stay a while.

For a Change

My anger is too much a lady
she does not shout
she sits in the corner and sulks.
I want to shake her, drag her out,
bring her into the light.

I want her to pummel her fists
on the table, make a noise,
I want her to wear lipstick
the colour of ripe plums
and dark roses
I want her to wear heels
and stamp her feet
I want her to be
a bitch –

but she will not oblige.

Trespasser

I have seen only his footprints
on the path early mornings,
but I know his eyes see me
through the tall blond grass.

Among the leaves,
his spots in dappled shade,
I imagine his green gaze
on my skin.

But here by the fountain
where the finches flutter,
hangs high
in the fork of a tree
the head of a Zebra.

Tonight we'll build a bigger fire.

Doodloop

Langs die stofpad staan jy
jou oë vriendelik verkreukel
in die middagson –
jy maak jou mond oop,
woorde kabbel uit soos klippertjies
in 'n vinnig vloeiende stroom –
sibilante sis en spat,
konsonante klap.
Ek vra na die pad
en jou vinger wys vêr
anderkant die heuwels.

Ek luister,
maar ek hoor net jou stem
en die wind in die gras –
ek kyk oor die veld,
maar my oë
kan jou tong se pad nie volg nie –
ek is verdwaal
in 'n doodloopgesprek
op 'n doodlooppad.

Klein-Karoo

Vanmôre soek ek
vroegoggend-sonskyn
op wit mure
'n tortelduif wat koer.
Karoodorp se stofstraat
gekeep deur spits skadus
van ou swart Sipresse.

Ek soek sonbesie-skreeu
al-om, al-om,
hulle besit mos die stilte,
moet dit uitbasuin.

Ek soek na leivore
koel, kabbelende strome
ek soek na elders
ek soek na iewers
waar ek kan sit,
voete in die water,
en binnetoe luister.

Wind sweep die wilgers,
klap die Karee
voor die stoep –
vaal stowwe warrel
wild deur die middag.
Die Klein-Karoolente
loop leeg
in duifblou berge.

Koel Karookamer
onder riet en balke,
buite die besies,
die bossies, die son –
hierbinne half-lig agter luike,
sing stilte en somer –
die blom van ledemate
ontvou in die soelte.

Rusplek

Soos uitgeknipte karton, ry op ry,
skuif die berge by die motorvenster verby,
pers-blou, grys-blou,
tot die bleekste blou van lug –
ons reis deur 'n land beroof van reën
waar populiere op plase
goud en amber fladder
en palmbome leun in die wind
lank en lankmoedig wuif hulle swart skadu's
oor eensame wit huise.
Die stofpad seil soos 'n slang
deur laagtes en oor riwwe van die voetheuwels –
vêr voor trek 'n motor 'n sleepsel stof
deur die namiddaghitte.

Vier ure vanaf die stad
laat my gemoed die rommel agter
om tevrede te neurie
in die bepeinsing van niks besonders nie
en hoe ek vannag sal slaap op 'n plek
waar sterre silwer lig spat
oor 'n swart fluweelnag

en waar die kerkklok
elke kwartier slaan –
elke kwartier van my lewe
wat oorbly.

Blind and Deaf, the Afternoon

SPRING

The first warmth of spring
sits comfortably on my shoulder,
the smell of pine and fynbos mingle
like a cocktail I would love to taste.
I am walking in the still plantation,
tree shadows fall in slanted spikes
across the sandy path.
The dogs run ahead,
turning dark, then bright,
into shadow, into light,
dry twigs snap, a hadedah objects
and screeches up into the blue.

7 MARCH 2016

Now at summer's end
the stream creeps underground
autumn dust hangs in the air,
the forest creaks – tinder-dry.
She leaves behind her
mother, sister, dog,
she runs ahead alone –
hell-bent, three shadows
fall across the sandy path.
No one sees
how they grab her –

↘

into shadow,
into that final night.
No one hears –
dry twigs snap,
only
a hadeda objects
and screeches up into the blue.

Oggendstap

Ek maak die hekkie
in die tuinmuur oop
op klam groen gras
waarin klein kolgansies
soos bont bolletjies dons
voor my voete wegskarrel
die stroom borrel
onder die houtbrug deur
skiet vonke
reënboog en diamant
oor die dwarswal se klippe
my hond gaan in
sak in die koel water neer
Piet-my-vrou loof die lente
vanuit ou bome
dit ruik na molm en aarde –

geen wierook hier of kerse
ek trap eerbiedig op dié grond
tussen hoë eike in.

The Modest Tree

Old and crooked
throughout the long wet winter
the oak tree wore its coat –
leaves of camel-brown,
but in spring when
lime-green shoots
shot out against the blue
it suddenly turned flashy,
changed into a flimsy frock.

When summer came
I sat in cool green shade
while cicadas screeched
their high-pitched song –
my world in order for a while.
Breakfasts and family feasts
were held beneath it,
it heard the children laugh.

I never saw it naked,
it was a modest tree –
the only one I hugged
when I left that house.

Yes or No?

Motionless
the tiny frog sits
between the petals of a rose –
I almost missed him
so small and pale
his bulging eyes stare in slits
into this springtime morning –
the only sign of life
just a throbbing heartbeat
at his throat.

Perhaps he's merely warming up
now that he's left his tadpole tail
back in the pond –
or perhaps he lingers
enchanted by the fragrance,
the apricot and amber
of his petalled cave.
He seems to be listening inwards.

Frog thoughts take time –
(some days even mine)
will he leap, or will he stay
a Buddha for a day?

Sun Moves

I like early morning sunlight,
the way it elbows through the trees
getting the birds all excited.
It smells of toothpaste,
toast and tea.
In passing, it caresses the cat,
but it is busy, there are things to do.

By mid-afternoon it slants into the room
dragging wearily across the dusty floor
like a tired friend hinting for a cup of tea –
who's come yet once again
to complain about life, its brevity.

By sunset thoughts turn
to evening dress –
to orange, lilac, purple
and that soft black velvet cloak.

Die blik vol knope

My ma het haar knope
in 'n blik gebêre –
hulle het my besig gehou
toe ek 'n klein maer dogtertjie was –
ek het sorteer, gekies,
rondes
rooies
pêrels
plattes.

Ek het die blik gehou –
soveel knope
wat nooit
weer aangewerk is nie
gekoop vir 'n rok
wat nooit gemaak is nie
of afgesny
van 'n geliefde kledingstuk
wat afgeleef was.

Nou sit ek
met 'n blik knope
op my skoot,
ek sorteer, ek kies,
probeer vind tussen
dowwes
vales
gebreektes

die blinkes.

Thirst

One warm day follows another
into what we used to call winter.
No rain falls,
dams dry up.

We buy bottled water,
hoard the plastic bottles
in cupboards like treasures –
the precious contents
to be rationed out
in the small blue glasses
for special occasions –
on that inconceivable day
when the taps
spit
only
air.

I also buy a string of glass beads
cold under my fingers
pale turqoise
like glacial ice.
I hang them
above the basin.

I touch them
to remind me
of water.

Dors

Een warm dag volg op die ander
tot in wat eens winter was.
Daar val geen reën nie,
damme droog op.

Ons koop gebottelde water,
stapel die plastiekbottels
in kaste soos skatte –
om die kosbare inhoud
te rantsoeneer
in die klein blou glasies
vir spesiale geleenthede –
op daardie ondenkbare dag
wanneer die krane
net
lug
spoeg.

Ek koop ook 'n string glaskrale,
koud onder my vingers,
bleek turkoois
soos gletser-ys.
Ek hang hulle
bo die wasbak.

Ek raak aan hulle
om my te herinner
aan water.

Writing in the Afternoon (A Pantoum)

My heart leaps up
my limbs are light
I write to remember
I write to forget

my limbs are light
I write mountains and molehills
I write to forget
the fear that fetters me

I write mountains and molehills
I write terror and tenderness
the fear that fetters me
a remnant of wholeness

I write terror and tenderness
I write to remember
a remnant of wholeness
my heart leaps up.

Miskien

Op daardie oggend
sal ek opswem
uit slaap
boontoe skop
uit 'n donker droom
na die lig daarbo,
die eerste asem
van die geel dag neem –
en besef:
alles het verander.

Maybe

On that morning
I shall swim up
from sleep
kick upwards
from a dark dream
to the light above,
draw the first breath
of the yellow day –
and realize:
everything has changed.

Vielleicht

An jenem Morgen
werde ich hochschwimmen
aus dem Schlaf
aufwärts treten
aus einem dunklen Traum
zu dem Licht oben,
den ersten Atemzug
des gelben Tages nehmen –
und begreifen:
Alles hat sich geändert.

The Lay of the Land

I'm leaving home today.
I'll travel far.
Until I can see
distant lightning
pointing out the place,
until I can hear
thunder's deep warning.
I'll take along
The Beatles or Beethoven,
depending on the route.

The smell of turpentine
will lead me there –
where the wind
blows fragrant promises
across the veld, the canvas
where my brush
may conjure clouds,
make rain.

Acknowledgements

Some of the poems in this collection have appeared in print elsewhere, in different languages and sometimes with different titles. My sincere thanks to the following publications:

Anthologies:
The Sol Plaatje European Union Poetry Anthology Vols. 2,3,4,5 and 7 (Jacana)
The McGregor Poetry Festival Anthology 2014 and *2016* ed. Patricia Schonstein (African Sun Press)
Absolute Africa ed. Patricia Schonstein (African Sun Press)
For Rhino in a Shrinking World ed. Harry Owen (The Poet's Printery)

Literary Magazines:
New Contrast
Stanzas

Online Magazines:
Type Cast

Thanks to Finuala Dowling for her poetry workshops, encouragement and commentary and to Karin Schimke for reading and commenting on the manuscript.

Thank you to my editor Danie Marais for meticulous and considered suggestions. Dit was 'n plesier om dwarsoor en dwarsdeur drie tale met jou saam te werk.

My gratitude and admiration goes to Colleen Higgs of Modjaji Books for the platform and space she continues to offer women writers in South Africa.

I thank my husband, my family and the many friends who have encouraged me.

You believed in me when I did not.

Author's Note

Where a poem appears in more than one language, the first version is not necessarily the original version. Poems were written in different languages as I felt the need to write them and all subsequent translations were done by me.

Printed in the United States
By Bookmasters